MEERKAT moves out of the DESERT

T0084480

by Nikki Potts • illustrated by Maarten Lenoir

PICTURE WINDOW BOOKS
a capstone imprint

Meerkats, meerkats
everywhere!

Pero las alas no son la única adaptación del halcón. Sus plumas también lo ayudan a volar y permanecer abrigado.
Su vista excelente, sus garras filosas y su pico curvado ayudan al halcón a atrapar y matar los pequeños animales que come.
Juntas, todas estas adaptaciones ayudan al halcón a sobrevivir en su hábitat.
ARDILLA VOLADORA
ACCESO AUTORIZADO: MAX AXIOM
¡Es un pájaro! ¡Es un avión! ¿Es una ardilla?
La ardilla voladora tiene un pliegue de piel que conecta las muñecas de las patas delanteras a los tobillos de las patas traseras. Este pliegue de piel ayuda a la ardilla a planear de rama a rama de árbol. Con un buen salto, las ardillas voladoras pueden planear de 20 a 30 pies por el aire.

Por supuesto, el estudio de la adaptación no es nada nuevo.
HMS BEAGLE
Visitemos a Charles Darwin. Algunas ideas importantes sobre la adaptación nacieron a partir de un viaje famoso marítimo que hizo en los 1830.
Hola, Sr. Darwin. ¿Va a explorar esa isla?
Sí. Es una de las Islas Galápagos. Estoy recolectando muchos especímenes, incluyendo aves, para llevar a Inglaterra.
GEOGRAFÍA
PACIFIC OCEAN
Las Islas Galápagos están a 600 millas al oeste de Ecuador, un país en Sudamérica.
Más adelante, Darwin se dio cuenta que los pinzones de las Galápagos tenían picos que se fueron adaptados a los alimentos de la isla que comían.
Darwin creía que los tipos especiales de picos se desarrollaron sobre el curso de muchos, muchos años.

Meerkats live together in burrows underground.

Baby meerkats. Mama meerkats. Daddy meerkats. Meerkat cousins.

Too many meerkats!

Meerkat wants some time alone. She needs her own place.

But where
should she go?
THIS WAY
OUT

The mountains!
It is much quieter here.

A little too quiet . . .

HELLOOOOOOOOOO!!!!

YIKES!
Meerkat has
caused an avalanche!

RUN!

Meerkat scurries as
fast as she can.

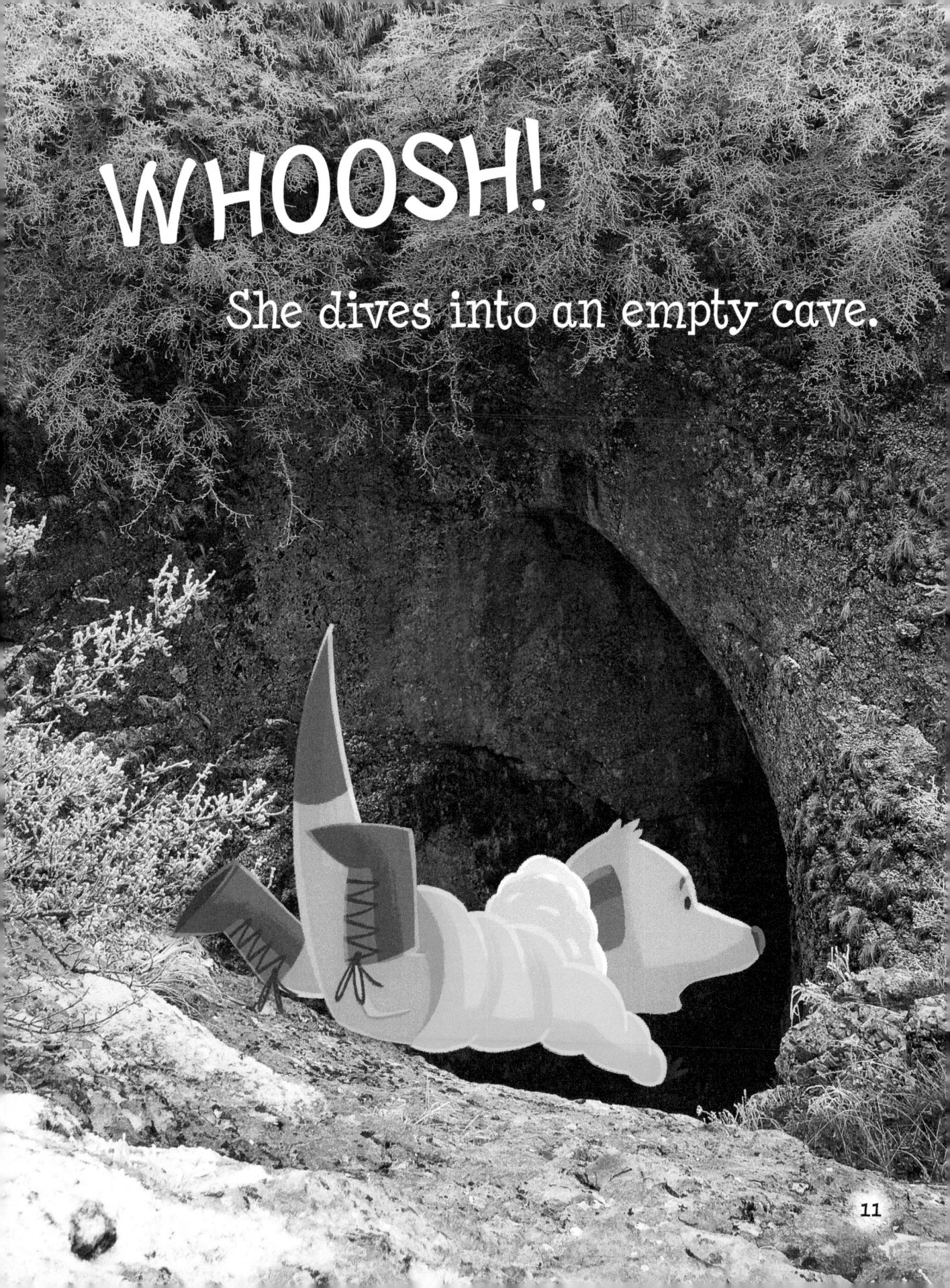
WHOOSH!
She dives into an empty cave.

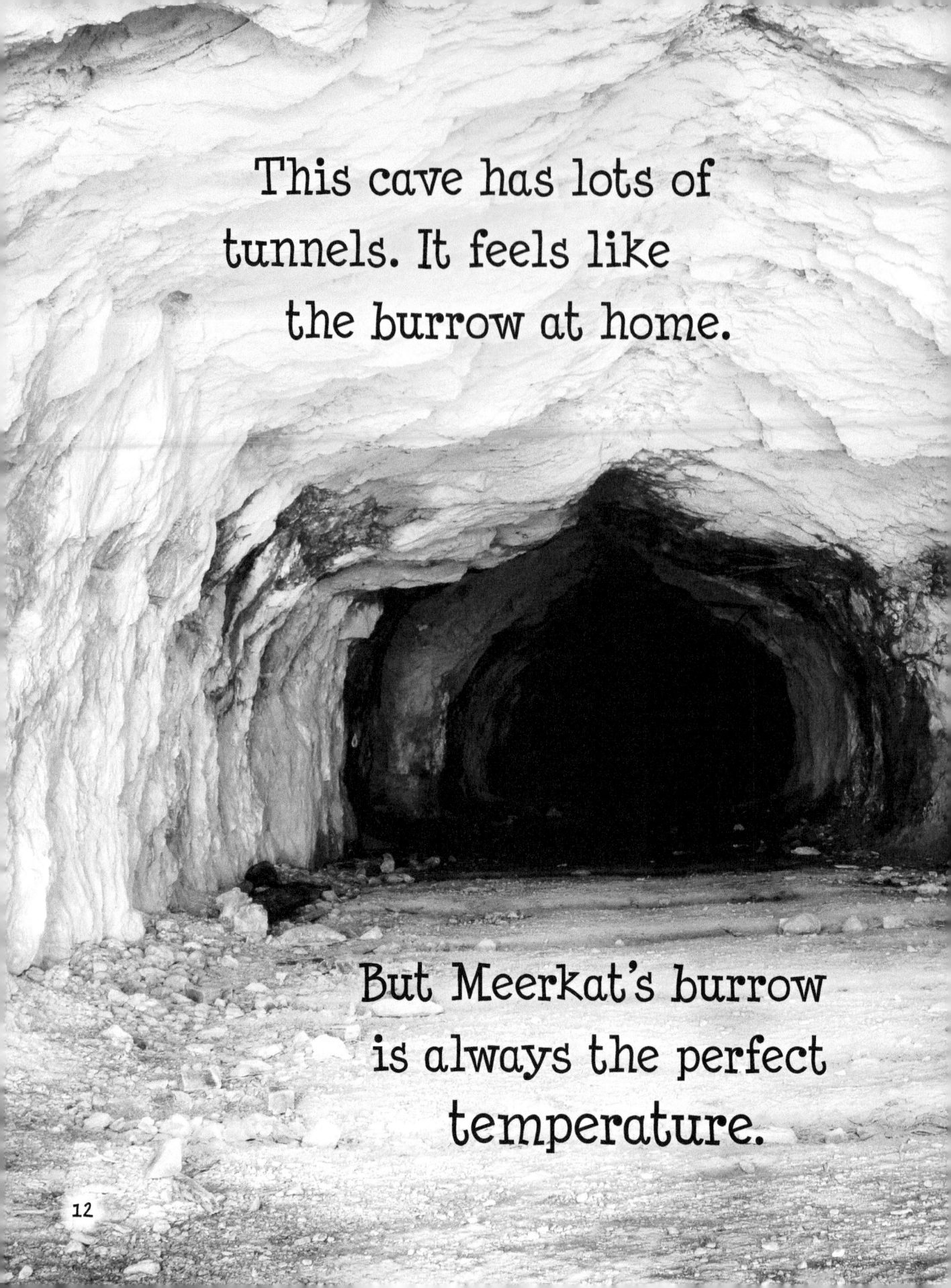

This cave has lots of tunnels. It feels like the burrow at home.

But Meerkat's burrow is always the perfect temperature.

Caves are much too cold.
BRRRR!

Meerkat thought
she was alone.
Then she
looked up.

Maybe she
can find a
new friend!

Meerkat is not ready
to make that many
new friends!

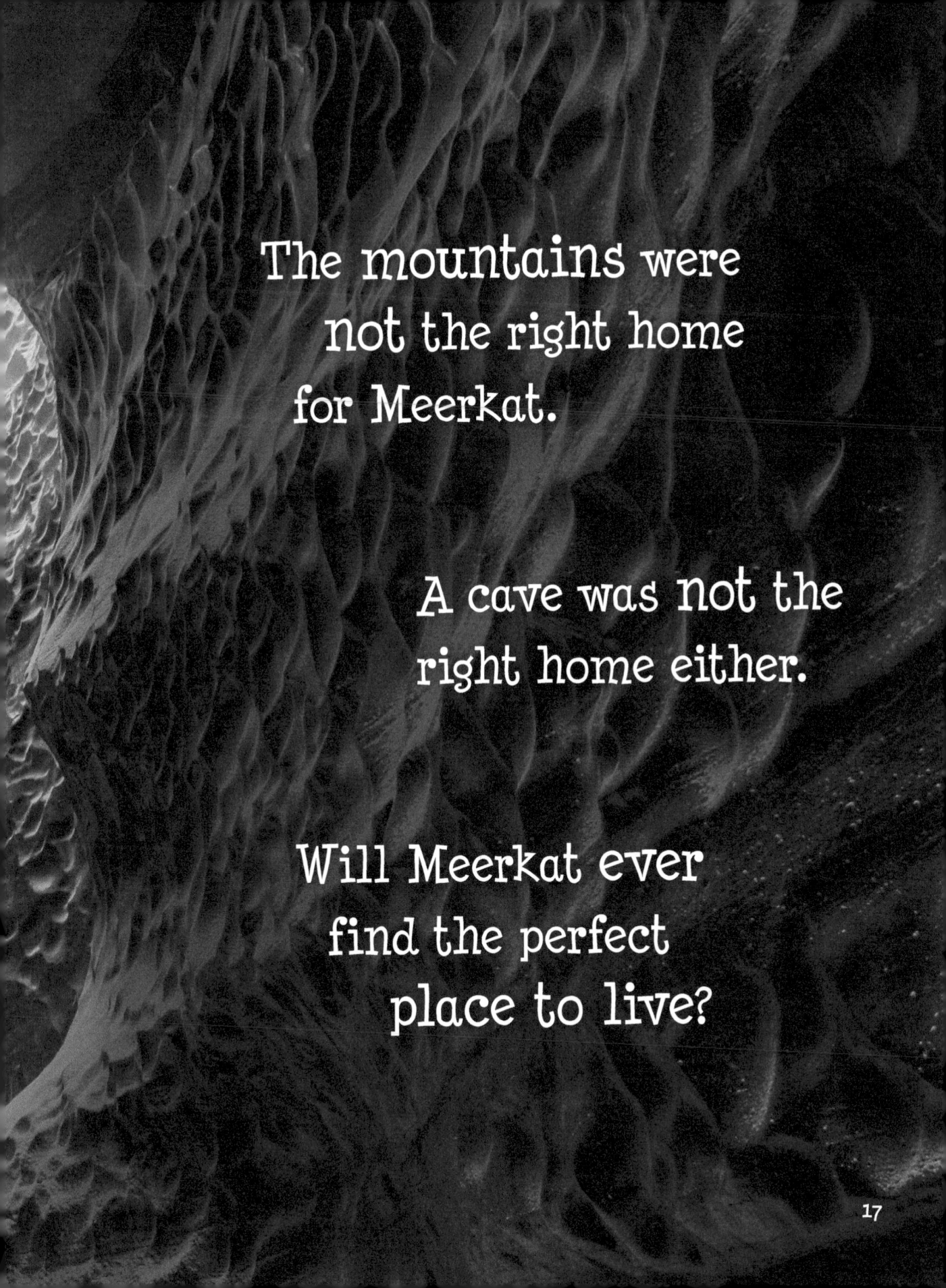

The mountains were not the right home for Meerkat.

A cave was not the right home either.

Will Meerkat ever find the perfect place to live?

WHEE!

Look at all these tunnels! This park could be the perfect place to live.

The monkey bars are too high!

OUCH!
The plastic slide is too hot!

This playground is
not the right habitat
for Meerkat.

Maybe a garden will be a nice place to live.

Now this is relaxing!

It is quiet here.
The plants are pretty.

There is plenty to eat.

And the dirt
is cool and soft.

Oh, no!

The dirt is TOO soft!

Meerkat cannot dig a burrow.

Without a burrow, how will Meerkat stay safe?

Meerkat misses the dry burrows.
She misses the hard dirt
that is perfect for tunneling.

She misses being warm.
She misses the noise.
Most of all, she misses
her family.

It is time
for Meerkat to
go home.

Everyone was waiting for Meerkat. That was a lot of waiting!

Welcome home, Meerkat!

ALL ABOUT MEERKATS

Meerkats only go outside during the day.

Meerkats have a very good sense of smell.

Adult meerkats take turns staying in the burrow to watch new pups.

Meerkat burrows have multiple entrances and exits.

A sentry is a meerkat who stands on a high point and watches for danger.

Meerkats hiss and show their teeth and claws when threatened.

ANIMAL PASSPORT

Name: Meerkat

Type: mammal

Habitat: desert

Diet: beetles, caterpillars, spiders, scorpions

Height: 11.4 inches (29 centimeters)

Weight: less than 2 pounds (1 kilogram)

Lifespan: 12 to 14 years

Favorite activity: cuddling

BOOKS IN THIS SERIES

Habitat Hunter is published by Picture Window Books, an imprint of Capstone.
1710 Roe Crest Drive
North Mankato, Minnesota 56003
www.capstonepub.com

Copyright © 2020 by Capstone. All rights reserved. No part of this publication may be reproduced in whole or in part, or stored in a retrieval system, or transmitted in any form or by any means, electronic, mechanical, photocopying, recording, or otherwise, without written permission of the publisher.

Library of Congress Cataloging-in-Publication Data is available on the Library of Congress website.
ISBN: 978-1-9771-1419-8 (library binding)
ISBN: 978-1-9771-2017-5 (paperback)
ISBN: 978-1-9771-1425-9 (eBook PDF)

Summary: Meerkat is bored with its habitat! Follow Meerkat as it tries out different places to live. Which habitat will make the best home for Meerkat?

Image Credits
Shutterstock: Albert Russ, 12-13, Alessio Bonfanti, 16-17, Alexander Raths, 26-27, Artography, 18-19, Fabio Lamanna, cover, Lysogor Roman, 8-9, My Good Images, 10, natali_polskaya, 26-27, Oleksii Grygorenko, 6-7, PandG, 24-25, Pasko Maksim, 22-23, r.kathesi, 14, RAJU SONI, 28-29, 31, reisegraf.ch, 15, senee sriyota, 20-21, shymar27, 4, skapuka, 14, Stacey Newman, 20 (inset), sumroeng chinnapan, cover, superbank stock, 14, tratong, 2-3, Vector8DIY, backcover, Yuriy Kulik, 11

Artistic elements: pingebat, Valeriya_Dor

Editorial Credits
Editor: Mari Bolte; Designer: Kayla Rossow; Media Researcher: Kelly Garvin; Production Specialist: Tori Abraham

All internet sites appearing in back matter were available and accurate when this book was sent to press.

Printed in the United States 5743